Bible Study Series
for junior high/middle school

THE TRUTH ABOUT THE Church

Loveland, Colorado

The Truth About the Church
Core Belief Bible Study Series
Copyright © 1998 Group Publishing, Inc.

All rights reserved. No part of this book may be reproduced in any manner whatsoever without prior written permission from the publisher, except where noted in the text and in the case of brief quotations embodied in critical articles and reviews. For information, write Permissions, Group Publishing, Inc., Dept. PD, P.O. Box 481, Loveland, CO 80539.

Credits
Editor: Karl Leuthauser
Creative Development Editors: Paul Woods and Ivy Beckwith
Chief Creative Officer: Joani Schultz
Copy Editors: Debbie Gowensmith and Candace McMahan
Art Director: Ray Tollison
Cover Art Director: Jeff A. Storm
Computer Graphic Artist/Illustrator: Eris Klein
Photographer: PhotoDisc
Production Manager: Gingar Kunkel

Unless otherwise noted, Scriptures quoted from the HOLY BIBLE, NEW INTERNATIONAL VERSION®. Copyright © 1973, 1978, 1984 by International Bible Society. Used by permission of Zondervan Publishing House. All rights reserved.

ISBN 0-7644-0899-2

10 9 8 7 6 5 4 3 2 1   07 06 05 04 03 02 01 00 99 98

Printed in the United States of America.

Bible Study Series
for junior high/middle school

contents:

the Core Belief: ▼ The Church

When anyone becomes a Christian, that person automatically becomes a part of the church, the body of Christ of which Christ is the head. Becoming a member of a church doesn't make a person a Christian. But all Christians can benefit from attending a local church. The local church provides opportunities for Christians to use the spiritual gifts the Holy Spirit gives them to edify the church and to help bring new people to Christ. The Holy Spirit often works through local churches to accomplish these purposes.

But church attendance isn't the goal for Christians. God designed the church as a body of people bringing the Good News to the world.

Today's young people need to discover that the church isn't a clique or a stale institution but a vital organism meant for bringing people into reconciliation with their Creator.

the ▼ Helpful Stuff

THE CHURCH AS A CORE CHRISTIAN BELIEF **7**
(or Why Your Body Needs to Be a Part of *the* Body)

ABOUT CORE BELIEF BIBLE STUDY SERIES **10**
(or How to Move Mountains in One Hour or Less)

WHY ACTIVE AND INTERACTIVE LEARNING WORKS WITH TEENAGERS **57**
(or How to Keep Your Kids Awake)

YOUR EVALUATION **63**
(or How You Can Edit Our Stuff Without Getting Paid)

the ▼Studies

Come As You Are   15
THE ISSUE: Unity
THE BIBLE CONNECTION: Romans 12:1-8 and 1 Corinthians 12
THE POINT: You can be part of Christ's body, the church.

Cyberfriends   25
THE ISSUE: Friendship
THE BIBLE CONNECTION: John 1:14; Acts 2:43-47; 4:32-35; Romans 1:10b-13; Ephesians 6:21-22; Hebrews 2:14-18; 4:14-16; and 1 John 1:1-4
THE POINT: You need real-life relationships in the church.

Resolution   35
THE ISSUE: Personal Conflicts
THE BIBLE CONNECTION: Matthew 5:21-26; 18:15-17
THE POINT: Sometimes Christians disagree.

The Power Within   45
THE ISSUE: Spiritual Gifts
THE BIBLE CONNECTION: Acts 8:26-40; 18:24-28; Ephesians 4:11-16; Hebrews 11:1-6; James 2:14-17; and 1 Peter 4:10-11
THE POINT: You have a gift to give.

The Church as a Core Christian Belief

Since its beginning, the church has survived every threat and onslaught that's come against it. Even now, two thousand years later, it continues to survive in the midst of hundreds of religions and philosophies around the globe. However, that doesn't mean the church has actually become the community God wants it to be—or that young people will automatically want to be a part of it. All too often, young people have seen the church marked by exclusion rather than by inclusion, by division rather than by unity, by rejection rather than by acceptance.

But that's precisely why kids need to learn about the true nature of the church. Each generation has to decide: Is the status quo good enough, or is it time to embrace Jesus' image of the church and let him turn it into a reality?

In the first study of this book, kids will learn how the people of God can look beyond their differences and work together toward common goals. They'll find ways to bring about God's plan of **unity** among all of his children as you remind them that they are a part of Christ's body.

The church is the one place where everyone should feel accepted and welcome. Use the second study to help kids explore what **friendship** within a church really means. You'll help them understand that they need real-life relationships that help them grow in faith.

Unity between churches seems impossible when there is so much disharmony *within* churches. The third study will show kids how to deal with **personal conflicts** and will simply remind them that sometimes Christians disagree. By learning to deal with conflict, kids will learn how to strengthen and bring healing to the church.

Your kids may lose sight of the important role and potential they have for the church. Don't let your kids be intimidated or ignored into apathy. Use the fourth study to show them how their **spiritual gifts** are very important to the life of the church and to remind them that they have a gift to give.

Your young people need the church. And the church needs your young people; their insight can help turn Jesus' image of the church into reality. Teaching your young people about the true nature of the church can help them transform your local body into the kind of loving community that Jesus spoke of two thousand years ago.

*For a more comprehensive look at this Core Christian Belief, read Group's **Get Real: Making Core Christian Beliefs Relevant to Teenagers.***

DEPTHFINDER: WHAT THE BIBLE TEACHES ABOUT THE CHURCH

To help you effectively guide your kids toward this Core Christian Belief, use these overviews as a launching point for a more in-depth study of the church.

- **New Testament writers speak of one general church and many local churches.** The general church includes every Christian. This general church finds its expression in local churches. A local church is any group of Christians in a particular place (Matthew 16:18; 1 Corinthians 4:17; Ephesians 1:22; Colossians 4:15).

- **Every Christian should invest in the local church.** The Holy Spirit has given every Christian a special ability to minister to other Christians. So we should invest in other Christians' lives on a regular basis to serve them and be served by them (Acts 2:41-47; 1 Corinthians 12:4-11; Ephesians 4:12-16; Hebrews 10:24-25).

- **Becoming a "member" of a church doesn't make you a Christian.** Only those who repent of their disobedience to God and personally trust Jesus Christ for the gift of eternal life are Christians and thus members of the general church (Matthew 7:13-23; Romans 3:21-25a; 6:23; 1 John 2:19).

- **The Holy Spirit created the church and empowers it for service.** The church was born shortly after Jesus' resurrection and ascension when the Holy Spirit descended on a group of Christians in Jerusalem. Since that day the Holy Spirit has empowered Christians to witness about Jesus and to minister to one another through the use of their spiritual gifts (Acts 1:8; 2:1-42; 1 Corinthians 12:4-13; Ephesians 4:4-13; 1 Peter 4:10-11).

- **Christ is the head of the church, which is his "body" in the world.** Christ, by means of the Holy Spirit, continues his earthly ministry through the church. Since each part of the body is necessary for the health and the growth of the whole, discrimination based on gender, race, spiritual gifts, or social status should be set aside (John 13:34-35; 15:17; Romans 12:4-8; Galatians 3:25-28; Ephesians 2:13-18; 4:1-6).

- **As the people of God, the church should be in the world but not of the world.** The Greek word for "church" refers to "a group of people called out or assembled." The church, then, consists of people called out of the world by God. However, that doesn't mean the church should isolate itself from the world. Instead, it is to remain in the world and make people disciples of Jesus (Matthew 28:18-20; John

17:14-19; 2 Corinthians 6:14–7:1; 1 Peter 2:9-10).
- **Since each Christian is a temple of the Holy Spirit, the church should promote holy living and true worship.** Christians should use the power of the Spirit to encourage Christian behavior in their own lives and the lives of others. This will enable the church to offer the true worship that arises from righteous living (John 4:23-24; 1 Corinthians 3:16-17; Galatians 5:22-23; Ephesians 2:21-22; 1 Peter 2:4-5).
- **As the bride of Christ, the church is destined for intimate union with him.** When Christ returns, the church will be united to him and will live and reign with him forever. In the meantime, the church is to remain loyal, pure, and ready for his return (2 Corinthians 11:2; Ephesians 5:25-27; 2 Timothy 2:11-13; Revelation 19:6-8; 20:6; 22:5).
- **Local churches should meet regularly for instruction, fellowship, prayer, worship, and the practice of the church's ordinances.** People learn about God and his will for their lives best when they study God's Word together. In addition, Christians can encourage one another, pray for individual and group needs, and praise God with one voice. Also, local churches should obey Christ by performing rites such as baptism and the Lord's Supper (Acts 2:41-42; 1 Corinthians 11:17-34; Ephesians 4:11-16; 1 Timothy 2:1-3; 4:13-16).
- **Local churches should follow the Holy Spirit's guidance to meet the physical needs of people around them.** Although it's important to tell others about Jesus and to build up other members of the church, that's not the church's only mission. The church should also meet people's physical needs regardless of whether they belong to the church. Among other things, the church should give food, clothing, and shelter to those who need it (Acts 2:43-45; Galatians 6:10; Hebrews 13:1-3, 16; James 1:27; 2:14-17; 1 John 3:16-18).

CORE CHRISTIAN BELIEF OVERVIEW

Here are the twenty-four Core Christian Belief categories that form the backbone of Core Belief Bible Study Series:

The Nature of God	Jesus Christ	The Holy Spirit
Humanity	Evil	Suffering
Creation	The Spiritual Realm	The Bible
Salvation	Spiritual Growth	Personal Character
God's Justice	Sin & Forgiveness	The Last Days
Love	The Church	Worship
Authority	Prayer	Family
Service	Relationships	Sharing Faith

Look for Group's Core Belief Bible Study Series books in these other Core Christian Beliefs!

about Core Belief Bible Study Series
for junior high/middle school

Think for a moment about your young people. When your students walk out of your youth program after they graduate from junior high or high school, what do you want them to know? What foundation do you want them to have so they can make wise choices?

You probably want them to know the essentials of the Christian faith. You want them to base everything they do on the foundational truths of Christianity. Are you meeting this goal?

If you have any doubt that your kids will walk into adulthood knowing and living by the tenets of the Christian faith, then you've picked up the right book. All the books in Group's Core Belief Bible Study Series encourage young people to discover the essentials of Christianity and to put those essentials into practice. Let us explain…

What Is Group's Core Belief Bible Study Series?

Group's Core Belief Bible Study Series is a biblically in-depth study series for junior high and senior high teenagers. This Bible study series utilizes four defining commitments to create each study. These "plumb lines" provide structure and continuity for every activity, study, project, and discussion. They are:

- **A Commitment to Biblical Depth**—Core Belief Bible Study Series is founded on the belief that kids not only *can* understand the deeper truths of the Bible but also *want* to understand them. Therefore, the activities and studies in this series strive to explain the "why" behind every truth we explore. That way, kids learn principles, not just rules.

- **A Commitment to Relevance**—Most kids aren't interested in abstract theories or doctrines about the universe. They want to know how to live successfully right now, today, in the heat of problems they can't ignore. Because of this, each study connects a real-life need with biblical principles that speak directly to that need. This study series finally bridges the gap between Bible truths and the real-world issues kids face.

- **A Commitment to Variety**—Today's young people have been raised in a sound bite world. They demand variety. For that reason, no two meetings in this study series are shaped exactly the same.

- **A Commitment to Active and Interactive Learning**—Active learning is learning by doing. Interactive learning simply takes active learning a step further by having kids teach each other what they've learned. It's a process that helps kids internalize and remember their discoveries.

For a more detailed description of these concepts, see the section titled "Why Active and Interactive Learning Works With Teenagers" beginning on page 57.

So how can you accomplish all this in a set of four easy-to-lead Bible studies? By weaving together various "power" elements to produce a fun experience that leaves kids challenged and encouraged.

- **A Relevant Topic**—More than ever before, kids live in the now. What matters to them and what attracts their hearts is what's happening in their world at this moment. For this reason, every Core Belief Bible Study focuses on a particular hot topic that kids care about.

- **A Core Christian Belief**—Group's Core Belief Bible Study Series organizes the wealth of Christian truth and experience into twenty-four Core Christian Belief categories. These twenty-four headings act as umbrellas for a collection of detailed beliefs that define Christianity and set it apart from the world and every other religion. Each book in this series features one Core Christian Belief with lessons suited for junior high or senior high students.

  "But," you ask, "won't my kids be bored talking about all these spiritual beliefs?" No way! As a youth leader, you know the value of using hot topics to connect with young people. Ultimately teenagers talk about issues because they're searching for meaning in their lives. They want to find the one equation that will make sense of all the confusing events happening around them. Each Core Belief Bible Study answers that need by connecting a hot topic with a powerful Christian principle. Kids walk away from the study with something more solid than just the shifting ebb and flow of their own opinions. They walk away with a deeper understanding of their Christian faith.

- **The Point**—This simple statement is designed to be the intersection between the Core Christian Belief and the hot topic. Everything in the study ultimately focuses on The Point so that kids study it and allow it time to sink into their hearts.

- **The Study at a Glance**—A quick look at this chart will tell you what kids will do, how long it will take them to do it, and what supplies you'll need to get it done.

Helpful Stuff   11

- **The Bible Connection**—This is the power base of each study. Whether it's just one verse or several chapters, The Bible Connection provides the vital link between kids' minds and their hearts. The content of each Core Belief Bible Study reflects the belief that the true power of God—the power to expose, heal, and change kids' lives—is contained in his Word.

THE POINT OF *BETRAYED!*:

God is love.

THE BIBLE CONNECTION
1 JOHN 4:7-21 — The Apostle John explains the nature and definition of perfect love.

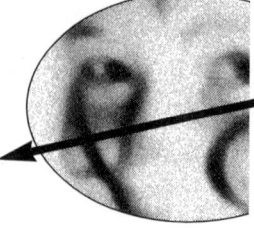

In this study, kids will compare the imperfect love defined in real-life stories of betrayal to God's definition of perfect love.

By making this comparison, kids can discover that God is love and therefore incapable of betraying them. Then they'll be able to recognize the incredible opportunity God of... relationship worthy of their absolute trust.

Explore the verses in The Bible Connection... mation in the Depthfinder boxes throughout... understanding of how these Scriptures connec...

THE STUDY

DISCUSSION STARTER ▼

Jump-Start (up to 5 minutes) As kids arrive, ask them to thin... common themes in movies, books, TV show... have kids each contribute ideas for a mast... two other kids in the room and sharing t... sider providing copies of People maga... what's currently showing on television... their suggestions, write their respon... come up with a lot of great idea... ent, look through this list and... ments most of these themes...

After kids make several su... responses are connected w... idea of betra...

● Why do you think betrayal is such a co...

Betrayed! 17

LEADER TIP for The Study
Because this topic can be so powerful and relevant to kids' lives, your group members may be tempted to get caught up in issues and lose sight of the deeper biblical principle found in The Point. Help your kids grasp The Point by guiding kids to focus on the biblical investigation and discussing how God's truth connects with reality in their lives.

DEPTHFINDER — UNDERSTANDING INTEGRITY

Your students may not be entirely familiar with the meaning of integrity, especially as it might apply to God's character in the Trinity. Use these definitions (taken from Webster's II New Riverside Dictionary) and other information to help you guide kids toward a better understanding of how God maintains integrity through the three expressions of the Trinity.

Integrity: 1. Firm adherence to a code or standard of values. 2. The state of being unimpaired. 3. The quality or condition of being undivided.

Synonyms for integrity include probity, completeness, wholeness, soundness, and perfection.

Our word "integrity" comes from the Latin word *integritas*, which means soundness. *Integritas* is also the root of the word "integer," which means "whole or complete," as in a "whole" number.

The Hebrew word that's often translated "integrity" (for example, in Psalm 25:21 [NIV]) is *tam*. It means whole, perfect, sincere, and honest.

CREATIVE GOD-EXPLORATION ▼

Top Hats (18 to 20 minutes) Form three groups, with each trio member from the previous activity going to a different group. Give each group Bibles, paper, and pens, and assign each group a different hat God wears: Father, Son, or Holy Spirit.
...their goal is to write one list describing what God does in the...

- **Depthfinder Boxes**—These informative sidelights located throughout each study add insight into a particular passage, word, historical fact, or Christian doctrine. Depthfinder boxes also provide insight into teen culture, adolescent development, current events, and philosophy.

Holy Profiles

Your assigned Bible passage describes how a particular person or group responded when confronted with God's holiness. Use the information in your passage to help your group discuss the questions below. Then use your flashlights to teach the other two groups what you discover.

■ Based on your passage, what does holiness look like?

■ What does holiness sound like?

■ When people see God's holiness, how does it affect them?

■ How is this response to God's holiness like humility?

■ Based on your passage, how would you describe humility?

■ Why is humility an appropriate human response to God's holiness?

■ Based on what you see in your passage, do you think you are a humble person? Why or why not?

■ What's one way you could develop humility in your life this week?

Permission to photocopy this handout from Group's Core Belief Bible Study Series granted for local church use.
Copyright © Group Publishing, Inc., Box 481, Loveland, CO 80539.

- **Leader Tips**—These handy information boxes coach you through the study, offering helpful suggestions on everything from altering activities for different-sized groups to streamlining discussions to using effective discipline techniques.

- **Handouts**—Most Core Belief Bible Studies include photocopiable handouts to use with your group. Handouts might take the form of a fun game, a lively discussion starter, or a challenging study page for kids to take home—anything to make your study more meaningful and effective.

The Last Word on Core Belief Bible Studies

Soon after you begin to use Group's Core Belief Bible Study Series, you'll see signs of real growth in your group members. Your kids will gain a deeper understanding of the Bible and of their own Christian faith. They'll see more clearly how a relationship with Jesus affects their daily lives. And they'll grow closer to God.

But that's not all. You'll also see kids grow closer to one another.

That's because this series is founded on the principle that Christian faith grows best in the context of relationship. Each study uses a variety of interactive pairs and small groups and always includes discussion questions that promote deeper relationships. The friendships kids will build through this study series will enable them to grow *together* toward a deeper relationship with God.

THE ISSUE: Unity

Come As You Are

Helping Kids Who Feel **Isolated** Find a Home at Church

by Stephen Parolini

■ Twelve-year-old Thomas doesn't spend much time with his friends anymore. Usually you'll find him in front of a television or his computer. On rare occasions, he'll be hiding behind a book. ■ It's not that Thomas isn't likable. He just doesn't feel connected with anyone. He'd rather live vicariously through the television characters shown daily on the eighty-three channels offered by his cable TV. ■ If one thing unites today's young people, it's the feeling of isolation that comes from growing up with a rising divorce rate and Walkman-type technologies. These kids desperately need a sense of belonging—a sense that comes from discovering they're an indispensable part of Christ's body, the church. ■ This study invites kids to discover that within the church, they can use their unique abilities to build vital relationships with one another and with Christ.

> **THE POINT:**
> You can be part of Christ's body, the church.

The Study AT A GLANCE

SECTION	MINUTES	WHAT STUDENTS WILL DO	SUPPLIES
Creative Opener	up to 5	WALKING TOGETHER—Try to find one interest common to everyone in the group.	
Individual Bible Exploration	20 to 25	ISOLATION—Call out things that isolate them as the leader moves them to different spots in the room.	Bibles, paper, pencils, "Isolation Assignments" handouts (p. 23)
Group Bible Exploration	20 to 25	BELONGING—Study Bible passages in groups and discuss how each group member contributed to the discussion.	Bibles, paper, pencils, "Isolation Assignments" handouts (p. 23), "Understanding the Church" Depthfinder (p. 20)
Closing	5 to 10	ESSENTIAL PARTS—Tell other students how they're important to the group.	

notes:

THE POINT OF *"COME AS YOU ARE"*:

You can be part of Christ's body, the church.

THE BIBLE CONNECTION

ROMANS 12:1-8; 1 CORINTHIANS 12 — Paul explains how each Christian has an essential role within the church.

In this study, kids will initially be isolated from one another and then will gradually become less isolated as they explore Scripture passages about their place in the church.

Through this experience, kids will learn that whatever their unique backgrounds, personalities, and abilities, they can be an indispensable part of Christ's body, the church.

Explore the verses in The Bible Connection; then study the information in the Depthfinder boxes throughout the study to gain a deeper understanding of how these Scriptures connect with your young people.

BEFORE THE STUDY

For every four students in your class, make one photocopy of the "Isolation Assignments" handout (p. 23). Cut apart the assignments as indicated by the dotted lines.

Make one photocopy of the "Understanding the Church" Depthfinder (p. 20) for each student.

LEADER TIP for The Study

Because this topic can be so powerful and relevant to kids' lives, your group members may be tempted to get caught up in issues and lose sight of the deeper biblical principle found in The Point. Help your kids grasp The Point by guiding kids to focus on the biblical investigation and by discussing how God's truth connects with reality in their lives.

LEADER TIP for The Study

Whenever groups discuss a list of questions, write the list on newsprint and tape the newsprint to a wall so groups can discuss the questions at their own pace.

LEADER TIP for Walking Together

When attempting to create a single group of people with the same interest, kids will probably form small groups first and then will try to combine those small groups. If they have difficulty finding a common interest, remind kids that they may have to start over again and call out new hobbies, sports, television programs, or other interests they have.

THE STUDY

CREATIVE OPENER ▼

Walking Together (up to 5 minutes)

As kids arrive, say: **Walk around the room calling out your interests, such as your favorite sport, hobby, television program, or movie. Keep calling out different interests until you find someone else who's calling out the same thing you're calling out. Then form a group with that person and anyone else who's calling out the same thing. Don't call out something just to form a group—be honest about your interests.**

After kids have formed a few groups, challenge kids to start the activity over with the goal of forming one big group. Explain that kids may have to call out a number of different interests to achieve this goal.

If the entire group finds one common interest, congratulate the kids. If kids are still searching after three minutes, stop the activity; then ask why it was difficult to find a common interest.

Then have kids form pairs to discuss these questions:

● **What new discovery did you make about someone through this activity?**

DEPTH FINDER — UNDERSTANDING THESE KIDS

Our society's ever-expanding technologies have both broadened and narrowed kids' worlds. Kids have immediate access to information, entertainment, and people of all kinds through their televisions, video games, and computers. They're beginning to see the bigness of their world.

Yet as kids grow more adept at navigating the technological maze, their social skills and real-life relationships diminish. Many of today's young people don't know how to reach out as friends, they don't know how to act in public, they feel uncomfortable sharing their feelings with others, and they don't know how to define and pursue dreams or goals.

Because of kids' diminishing social abilities and friendships, ministering to this generation means helping kids to develop real-life relationships. You can begin by learning about your kids' technological world. For example, play a video game with them or let them show you what they're discovering about the world and people through their online adventures. Then provide opportunities for kids to meet face to face in small groups, such as taking three or four of them to lunch. Through this interaction, your students will begin to learn about real-life relationships. And through these real-life relationships, your students can discover how to build a relationship with Jesus Christ.

- **Why did it take so long** (or so little time) **for us to find common ground?**
- **How does this activity reflect both our unity and our individuality?**

Say: **While this activity shows us how we have some common interests, it also shows us how diverse we are. In many ways, our similarities and differences are the trademarks of the church. We share common beliefs about Christ, but we build our relationships with Christ in different ways, using different gifts and abilities. Today we'll explore how <u>you can be part of Christ's body, the church.</u>**

INDIVIDUAL BIBLE EXPLORATION ▼

Isolation (20 to 25 minutes) Have everyone stand close together in the center of the room. Say: **Sometimes our differences separate us. But other things also cause us to feel alone or isolated. These feelings make it difficult for us to find a home in a group such as the body of Christ, the church.**

Have kids call out things that separate them from friends, family, church, and God. For example, kids might say things like "different interests," "lack of quality time with parents," "disagreements with friends," "television," or "distractions like video games."

As kids call out these ideas, randomly choose a student and physically guide that student toward any of the classroom's walls. Then choose another student to move. Continue this until all students are standing, facing the walls, with plenty of room between them. If you

"Just as each of us has **one body** with many members, and these members do not all have the same function, so in Christ we who are many form one body, and each member belongs to all the others."

—Romans 12:4-5

LEADER TIP for Isolation

Your students may clam up as you move them away from each other, or they may insist on talking with each other when they're supposed to spend time alone. You can view these responses as resistance to isolation and use them to your advantage. If kids respond in these ways, stop what you're doing, and ask:
- Why do you become silent as I move you away from each other?
- Why do you talk when you're supposed to spend time alone?
- How does being isolated make you feel?
- Why is being isolated so hard?

LEADER TIP for Isolation

During this activity, discreetly offer help to any kids who have trouble finding their assigned Bible passages.

LEADER TIP for Isolation

If you have a large group or a small meeting room that prohibits you from adequately isolating kids along the perimeter of the room, isolate kids into two or more concentric circles.

have another adult volunteer, have him or her help you move the kids. If kids run out of things to say before you've moved everyone, have students describe times they've felt isolated.

Give each student a sheet of paper and a pencil. Say: **It's hard to feel that we belong anywhere when so many things isolate us from people we care about. In our next activity, you'll discover how you can be part of Christ's body, the church. I'm going to lead us in a prayer; after I pray, say in unison, "Show us how we're part of your body, the church. Amen."**

Pray aloud: **Dear God, sometimes we feel so alone. But you've created a body of people meant to work together—your church.** Lead the group in praying: **Show us how we're part of your body, the church. Amen.**

After the prayer, have kids write their own definitions of "church" on their papers. As kids do this, hand each student a Bible and one of the assignments from the "Isolation Assignments" handout (p. 23). Be sure to distribute the assignments evenly among group members. Tell kids to do their assignments without help from anyone else. Kids may use their papers to write notes about their discoveries.

GROUP BIBLE EXPLORATION ▼

Belonging (20 to 25 minutes)

Have kids form four groups according to which assignment they completed from the handout. In these groups, have kids share their definitions of "church" and their reactions to the assignment.

DEPTHFINDER — UNDERSTANDING THE CHURCH

How do you define the word "church"? When some people hear that word, the first thing they envision is a building. Others think of a group of people who live as a community with one another. Here are some Scriptures that help us understand this second definition of church:

- **Acts 2:42-47**—The church is a fellowship of Christians who worship together, reach out to others, spend time together, and take care of each other.
- **1 Corinthians 12:27-31**—The church is a group of people who each contribute unique gifts to the whole group.
- **2 Corinthians 6:4-10**—Church members must serve God and his people.
- **Ephesians 2:22**—The church is a group of believers inhabited by God through his Holy Spirit.
- **Colossians 1:18**—Jesus Christ is the head of the church.
- **1 Thessalonians 4:9-10**—People in the church must love one another.
- **1 Timothy 3:14-15**—The church is God's family.
- **1 Peter 2:4-5**—People become part of the church when they commit themselves to Jesus Christ.

Permission to photocopy this Depthfinder from Group's Core Belief Bible Study Series granted for local church use. Copyright © Group Publishing, Inc., P.O. Box 481, Loveland, CO 80539.

Come As You Are   20

DEPTHFINDER: UNDERSTANDING THESE KIDS

Listed below are five ways to help kids feel like they belong to the church community.

1. Give kids real responsibilities instead of token ones. Consider having kids join decision-making committees or help lead worship by reading Scripture, playing music, or sharing life stories that relate to the sermon.

2. Help kids find ways to make a difference in their world. Because today's kids have few national causes to support or fight, they often feel they have no impact on the world. Today's young people favor impacting people on a smaller scale—making a difference in the lives of those they come into contact with on a daily basis. Give your students opportunities to reach others right where they live, such as serving a meal in a homeless shelter or creating a day camp for neighborhood children.

3. Downplay the idea of the church as an institution. Kids who feel ownership in their church's mission will more actively participate in church than kids who constantly hear that their church requires attendance, tithes, and participation. Foster teenagers' ownership in the church by following the first idea on this list and taking seriously their suggestions, concerns, ideas, and dreams for the church.

4. Teach kids the basics. Raised in a world of relativism, today's kids need to understand that some absolutes exist. However, teaching absolutes to kids who don't believe in them is a challenge. Help kids understand the basics of faith as they apply it to their own lives. When your students grasp these fundamentals for themselves, help them see how these truths affect everyone.

5. Be yourself. Kids have little patience for people who try to be like them in order to reach them. They appreciate honesty (even when it's a little painful or gritty) far more than attempts to "reach their level." Speak from your own experiences and be yourself as you minister to your kids. They'll discover that the church consists of real people with real needs and real love for one another.

(Adapted from "The Gospel for Generation X" by Dieter Zander, Christianity Today, Inc./ Leadership Journal, 1995, from America Online.)

After five minutes, have kids form groups of four that include one member from each assignment group. Tell kids to share what they discovered through their individual study and in their assignment groups. Be sure each group member shares at least one insight from the previous study and discussion.

Then have foursomes discuss these questions:
- **What is a definition of "church" that you can all agree on?**
- **How was the way you learned about the Bible passages like the way the church works? How was it different?**
- **How do the Scripture passages apply to our group?**
- **How do we each fill a unique place in the group?**
- **When we each fill a unique place, how are we fulfilling what Paul says about people's roles in the body of Christ?**
- **How is our group like one body?**

Give kids copies of the "Understanding the Church" Depthfinder (p. 20). Have kids read the Depthfinder, including the passages listed, to revise their definitions of "church." Have each group read its revised definition to the rest of the class.

Then have foursomes discuss these questions:
- **What did you discover in today's activities about learning in isolation and in groups?**
- **How was the way you each contributed something unique to the group discussions like the way each person contributes something unique to our group? to your school? to your family? to the church?**
- **How have you experienced people in this group and in our church using gifts such as the ones Paul listed in Romans 12:1-8 and 1 Corinthians 12?**
- **What gifts do you think God has given you? How has God used your gifts?**

Say: **Just as all of you played important and unique roles in this Bible exploration, <u>you can be part of Christ's body, the church.</u> When you begin a lifelong relationship with Jesus Christ, the Holy Spirit gives you unique and divine abilities that the church needs you to use.**

CLOSING ▼

Essential Parts (5 to 10 minutes)

Have kids brainstorm a list of four common items such as a bicycle, a computer, a blow-dryer, and a lawn mower. Encourage kids to consider items that have a lot of parts and serve specific purposes.

Then have each person choose which item he or she most feels like. Have kids form groups based on the items they most identify with. For example, all the kids who feel like a bicycle should form one group. Make sure there are at least two people in each group. Then have kids tell their group members why they feel like the item they chose. For example, a student might say, "I feel like a computer today because I have a lot of homework to do."

Ask each group to form a circle. Beginning with a person you designate, have each person describe the essential function the person to his or her right would perform in the group's item. For example, someone in the lawn mower group might say, "Sarah is like a mower blade because she is so good at getting things done. She cuts right to the point." Remind kids to be positive and to think in terms of how the people on their right contribute to the group and to the church.

Then say: **We each play a different role in this group and in all the groups we belong to. And just as each of you is an essential part of this group, <u>you can be part of Christ's body, the church.</u> But unlike other groups you're in, when you're in the body of Christ, you're never alone again. Even when other Christians aren't around, God is always with you.**

Before kids leave, challenge them each to think of one way they can use their gifts in the coming week. Encourage kids who want to know more about being a Christian to talk to you and, if possible, to another student who's a mature Christian.

Come As You Are   22

Isolation Assignments

Assignment 1: Figure out how Romans 12:1-8 applies to your life today.

Assignment 2: Read Romans 12:1-8 and determine what Paul was saying to the early Christians about their roles in the church.

Assignment 3: Read 1 Corinthians 12 and figure out how the Scripture might apply to our group members' roles in church today.

Assignment 4: Read 1 Corinthians 12 to discover what Paul was saying to the early Christians about spiritual gifts.

THE ISSUE: Friendship

CYBER FRIENDS

Building Real-Life Relationships in @n Online World

<by Lisa Baba Lauffer>

⌨ The click of computer keys. Words on a screen. Electronic pulses that travel from computer to computer. ⌨ These are the components of an online relationship. ⌨ More and more young people are "surfin' the Net" these days, making friends across the continents through e-mail, chat rooms, and message boards. Without leaving their homes, many kids can share their views, learn about others, and explore the world. ⌨ But how do they know when they've really connected with others? Are their needs for friendship really being met? ⌨ This study invites kids to experience an "online" world and then evaluate what it can and cannot give them. Through this study, your young people can discover their need for a community of real-life friends they can see, hear, and touch.

THE POINT: You need real-life relationships in the church.

The Study AT A GLANCE

SECTION	MINUTES	WHAT STUDENTS WILL DO	SUPPLIES
Setup	10 to 15	**LOGGING ON**—Create their own screen names and learn the guidelines for the study.	Bibles, adhesive name tags, slips of paper, pens, box, masking tape, scratch paper, "Rules for Online Interaction" handouts (p. 32), "My Online Friend" handouts (p. 33)
Computer Simulation	30 to 35	**ONLINE RESEARCH**—Try to learn about someone else in the room without talking directly to him or her and then explore Scriptures about having real-life relationships.	Bibles, "Rules for Online Interaction" handouts (p. 32), "My Online Friend" handouts (p. 33), scratch paper, newsprint, marker, masking tape
Friendship Evaluation	5 to 10	**DOWNLOADING INFORMATION**—Compare the quality of online relationships to real-life relationships and scriptural guidelines for friendships.	Bibles, "My Online Friend" handouts (p. 33)
	up to 5	**VIRTUALLY ENCOURAGING**—Write affirmations about the people they learned about during the "Online Research" activity.	"My Online Friend" handouts (p. 33), pens

notes:

THE POINT OF "CYBERFRIENDS":

You need real-life relationships in the church.

THE BIBLE CONNECTION

JOHN 1:14; HEBREWS 2:14-18; 4:14-16; 1 JOHN 1:1-4	These passages describe the impact of Jesus' becoming human to develop relationships with us.
ACTS 2:43-47; 4:32-35	These passages explain how the first church developed relationships and met each other's needs.
ROMANS 1:10b-13; EPHESIANS 6:21-22	Paul expresses how much it meant to him to visit his brothers and sisters in Christ.

In this study, students will try to learn about other students in the group by interacting with them through "message boards" and "chat rooms."

By simulating computer relationships, kids can realize that they need friends they can see, hear, and touch.

BEFORE THE STUDY

Write each of the following sentences across the top of a separate sheet of newsprint:

What do you believe about God? What's your favorite color? Who has been the most important person in your life? If you could do anything, without any restrictions on your time or money, what would you do? What's the best thing about being in this youth group? What's the worst thing? What do you think are the most important qualities of a friend? What scares you more than anything else? Do you have a scar? If so, where? What's the best advice you could give someone about being a friend? Where's the most unusual place you've ever been? What do you think the Bible says about having computer relationships? What's the silliest thing you've ever done with a friend?

Tape each sheet of newsprint to a wall at a level where kids will be able to write on it.

Make ten photocopies of the "Rules for Online Interaction" handout (p. 32), and tape the photocopies to the walls so kids can refer to them during the study.

Create a masking tape circle on the floor in the center of the room. Make the circle big enough to fit six of your students at a time.

LEADER TIP for The Study

Because this topic can be so powerful and relevant to kids' lives, your group members may be tempted to get caught up in issues and lose sight of the deeper biblical principle found in The Point. Help your kids grasp The Point by guiding kids to focus on the biblical investigation and by discussing how God's truth connects with reality in their lives.

Cyberfriends 27

THE STUDY

SETUP ▼

Logging On (10 to 15 minutes)

Leader Tip for Logging On

Some of your kids (and your adult volunteers!) may not be familiar with online resources. To help kids understand the study topic, explain some of the terms described in the "Understanding the Online World" Depthfinder (p. 29). Or have one of your students who's a computer expert explain what's available online.

When kids have arrived, say: **Today we're going "online" to discover more about each other. This room will be our "computer." Before we begin our online experience, think of a "screen name" for yourself. Be creative! Your name can reflect anything about you, such as "SkiBum" or "Luv2Read."** When kids have thought of their names, have each student write the name on both an adhesive name tag and a slip of paper. Then have kids put their name tags on themselves and put their slips of paper in a box.

Have kids form groups of four. Set out masking tape and say: **Before we go online, your group needs to create a "private chat room." During the study, you and your "chat mates" will meet in this private chat room for discussion, so make it a place you want to be. Use the masking tape to create a room. You can make your room any shape, such as a star or a triangle. Make sure that all four chat mates can sit in it comfortably. Then place your Bibles in your chat room so you can use them during the study.**

When groups have finished creating their private chat rooms, hand each student a small stack of scratch paper and a pen. Say: **Your task today is to get to know someone in this class better. You'll pick a screen name from the box, and I'll give you a handout that lists things you need to learn about that person. However, there are specific rules for using our computer.** Read aloud the "Rules for Online Interaction" handout (p.32).

When everyone understands the activity, give each person a copy of the "My Online Friend" handout (p. 33). Have each student pick a screen name from the box, making sure to not pick his or her own name or the name of a chat mate. Say: **We're ready to begin now, so log on and do your research about the person whose screen name you picked! As you participate in this activity, think of your opinion about this statement: <u>You need real-life relationships in the church.</u>**

COMPUTER SIMULATION ▼

Leader Tip for Online Research

When you want to get kids' attention for the "system failures," use a whistle or a bell.

Online Research (30 to 35 minutes)

Allow kids to walk around the room, respond to the message boards, and begin to learn about the people whose screen names they picked. If kids breach any guidelines for the

Cyberfriends 28

study, be the "system monitor" and gently remind them of the rules.

After seven minutes, say: **System failure! Return to your private chat rooms while I fix the computer.** Then have foursomes discuss these questions:

● **What's your reaction to communicating with others in this way?**

● **What have you learned about your person so far?**

● **How is this experience showing you that <u>you need real-life relationships in the church</u>?**

● **Read John 1:14; Hebrews 2:14-18; 4:14-16; and 1 John 1:1-4. What do these passages say about why Jesus became human?**

● **How does Jesus' coming to earth as a human reflect how <u>you need real-life relationships in the church</u>?**

● **So far, how is this experience affecting what you think about having online and real-life relationships?**

When groups have finished discussing the questions, say: **I almost have the computer fixed. While I finish up, pray with your chat mates. Pray that God will teach you, through Jesus' example, how <u>you need real-life relationships in the church.</u>**

DEPTH FINDER
UNDERSTANDING THE ONLINE WORLD

Today's generation of kids is characterized by its access to and familiarity with online resources. Most kids can easily navigate their way through the electronic maze, but you may feel lost and bewildered.

Here are some of the resources that are available online:

● **E-mail**—A system allowing people to send each other messages from computer to computer.

● **Chat rooms**—Places where people can type messages to each other in "real time" (almost instantaneously). These rooms hold a number of people, and people who "chat" with each other can also send each other private "instant messages."

● **Message boards**—Places where people can post questions or statements for others to respond to. Responses to message and bulletin boards are available for anyone to read.

● **Multi-User Dungeons (MUDs)**—Electronic games in which people create alternative identities and use words to play interactive computer games. Some of these games have evil undertones and are as addictive to young people as Dungeons and Dragons.

Online resources are like many other resources; whether they're good or bad depends on how people use them. Your young people can use their computers to gain access to magazines, encyclopedias, and other information they can use for learning. However, they also have access to pornography and sex talk. Through chat rooms and e-mail, they're vulnerable to people who don't have their best interests at heart.

You can help your kids make good online choices by evaluating their online activities with them. Also encourage parents to monitor their kids' online involvement.

LEADER TIP
for Online Research

Since this experience is somewhat unstructured, kids may take liberties with the freedom you've given them. To bring some control back into the study, you may call a system failure at any time. Here are some questions you can ask during these impromptu system failures:

● Have you been tempted to talk directly with your online person? Explain.

● What's the most interesting thing you've found out about your online friend?

● How is the mayhem in this room like trying to get to know someone online?

● Have you ever gotten to know someone online? If so, how does that friendship compare with your real-life friendships?

● How can the church meet your need for real-life relationships?

● Who is one real-life friend that you value? Why?

● What is one thing you can do for a real-life friend to deepen your friendship?

Ask one or two of these questions during each impromptu system failure. When kids settle down, let them continue their online research.

LEADER TIP for The Study

Whenever groups discuss a list of questions, write the list on newsprint and tape the newsprint to a wall so groups can discuss the questions at their own pace.

DEPTH FINDER — UNDERSTANDING THE BIBLE

God can often seem like a connection on the Internet—in most cases we can't see, touch, or hear him, but we know he's there. Jesus became a human to reveal to us God the Father. John 1:18 says, "No one has ever seen God, but God the One and Only, who is at the Father's side, has made him known." The Disciple's Study Bible asserts that Jesus Christ "revealed the fullness of God's identity in flesh. The glory of God...became visible as grace and truth which all people need...He is God in flesh letting us see what otherwise was impossible to see."

When groups have finished praying, say: **We're up and running again. You may proceed with your research about your online friend.**

Allow kids to continue their research.

After seven minutes have elapsed, say: **System failure! Return to your foursomes to discuss these questions:**

● **Read Acts 2:43-47 and 4:32-35. How did the church members in these Bible passages relate to each other?**

● **What can you learn from the early church about your need for real-life relationships?**

● **How can our church today meet the needs of church members as the members of the church in Acts met each other's needs?**

● **What's one way you'll begin to build a real-life relationship within our church or our youth group?**

When groups have finished discussing the questions, say: **In your groups, pray that God will use the example of the early church to show you how <u>you need real-life relationships in the church</u>.**

Then say: **I was able to fix the computer only temporarily. It will shut down in one minute, so use that time to find out any last-minute information about your person.**

When one minute has elapsed, say: **The computer is now shut down, and you now may communicate with each other as you usually do. In the next activity, we'll discuss our online experience.**

FRIENDSHIP EVALUATION ▼

Downloading Information (5 to 10 minutes) Gather kids together and see who got the most information about his or her online person. If you have ten or fewer students, have all the kids read their answers aloud and see how much of the information they got is correct. If you have more than ten students, have kids meet with their online friends and figure out how much information they got right. If students got any information wrong or had blanks left to fill, have them make those adjustments.

Then have groups meet in their private chat rooms to discuss these questions:
- **Which method of getting to know each other did you like better—the online way or through direct discussion? Explain.**
- **How is directly asking for information like what we learned about relationships in the Bible passages we read earlier?**
- **What have you learned today about having online relationships? real-life relationships?**
- **Read Romans 1:10b-13 and Ephesians 6:21-22. How do these passages show Paul's need for real-life relationships?**
- **How was Paul's need for real-life relationships like your need for real-life relationships?**
- **How can you seek real-life relationships in the church?**
- **How can we in this room meet each other's needs for real-life relationships?**

Say: **Online friendships are good friendships, and they're really fun. But you need friends you can see, hear, and touch. It makes a difference to have people, especially church friends, who you can hug, tap on the shoulder, listen to, and talk to. You need real-life relationships in the church.**

Virtually Encouraging (up to 5 minutes)

Say: **One way we can enhance our real-life relationships, especially in the church, is by encouraging each other.** Have kids turn their "My Online Friend" handouts over and write on the back reasons they're glad to have real-life relationships with their "online" friends in the class. For example, they may write, "I'm glad we have a real-life relationship because your smile encourages me." Then have kids give their handouts to their online friends.

Before kids leave, have them share with their online friends ways they'll pursue real-life relationships during the week. For example, a student can commit to inviting a friend to get ice-cream cones or to calling someone he or she hasn't spoken to for a while.

<Rules for Online Interaction>

1. You may not talk directly to anyone.

2. You may learn things about people by reading their responses on the "message boards" around the room—the sheets of newsprint with questions for all of you to respond to.

3. The only time you may write directly to your person is if you and the person whose name you picked are in the "chat room"– the circle of masking tape in the center of the room. To "chat" with that person, you must coax him or her into the chat room, write your question on your scratch paper, allow your person to read the question and write an answer, and then leave. You may ask only one question each time you're in the chat room.

4. After you've been in a chat room, you must go to a message board to either write or read a response.

5. Only six people may be in the chat room at a time.

6. At the beginning, you must write responses on at least three message boards. Then you may start learning about your person.

7. You may write on a message board any time you wish.

8. Whenever you write on a message board, you must sign your screen name.

9. By the end of our online experience, you must write on at least nine of the message boards.

10. While you're online, there may be "system failures." If the leader calls out, "System failure!" you must return to your private chat room and discuss with your chat mates the questions the leader asks.

My Online Friend

Use the message boards and the chat room to find out the following things about your online friend:

- one of your friend's dreams for the future
- your friend's deepest fear
- what your friend's relationship with God is like
- the most important person in your friend's life
- your friend's favorite amusement park ride
- your friend's feelings about school
- the farthest place from here that your friend has been
- your friend's favorite sport (if he or she likes sports)
- your friend's favorite breakfast cereal
- what your friend likes and/or dislikes about online relationships
- what your friend values about friendship
- whether your friend has a scar and where
- the family member your friend is closest to
- the length of time your friend has been involved in our group
- the flavor of ice cream your friend has most recently tasted

THE ISSUE: Personal Conflicts

RESOLUTION

HELPING KIDS DEAL WITH CONFLICT

by Tim Baker

■ Isn't it nice to know that when you become a Christian, all your problems go away? Things become perfect. No quarrels. No disagreements. Harmony. Peace. Unity. No problems with other Christians. No worries about difficulties with other people. ■ Wrong. ■ As long as you have relationships, you will have conflict. Being a Christian doesn't change that fact. You can apply Christian principles, but you'll still run into differing opinions, disagreements, and outright arguments. ■ This study zeroes in on dealing with conflict. It will help your kids talk about how conflict makes them feel. It will help them work through conflict-resolution steps and discover what God's Word says about conflict. But most importantly, this study will help your kids see that even though they might be Christians, they will still have to work through conflict.

THE POINT:

Sometimes Christians disagree.

The Study AT A GLANCE

SECTION	MINUTES	WHAT STUDENTS WILL DO	SUPPLIES
Expressive Opening	5 to 10	THE BIG FIGHT—Observe their friends in a "real-life" conflict.	
	10 to 15	FIGHT FEELIN'—Use mud to make a mural that represents how conflict makes them feel.	Mud, plastic containers, newsprint, water, soap, paper towels
Kinetic Exploration	20 to 30	STEP INTO CONFLICT—Prepare skits to demonstrate ways to deal with conflict.	Bibles, "Conflict Scenarios" handouts (p. 42), paper, pens, yarn, scissors, "Resolution" handouts (p. 43)
	5 to 10	TANGLED UP IN CONFLICT—Use yarn to discuss a conflict that they've had.	Bible, balls of yarn, scissors

notes:

THE POINT OF "RESOLUTION":

Sometimes Christians disagree.

THE BIBLE CONNECTION

MATTHEW 5:21-26   Jesus orders Christians to reconcile conflict with others.

MATTHEW 18:15-17   Jesus describes how we should approach another Christian who has sinned against us.

In this study, kids will discuss a staged argument, use mud to create murals that represent how they feel when they have a conflict, prepare skits to demonstrate ways to deal with conflict, and use yarn to illustrate conflicts they've had.

Through these experiences, your kids can learn to recognize conflict and gain valuable tools for dealing with it.

Explore the verses in The Bible Connection; then examine the information in the Depthfinder boxes throughout the study to gain a deeper understanding of how these Scriptures connect with your young people.

BEFORE THE STUDY

For "The Big Fight" ask two kids to stage a verbal fight at the beginning of your meeting. Instruct one student to take the chair of the other student. Ask your actors to argue loudly and realistically over who gets the chair. Arrange a signal, such as blowing your nose, that others won't notice. Tell the actors to wait for your signal before they begin. Be sure to remind them that they're not to be physically violent or profane.

For "Fight Feelin' " fill one small plastic container with mud for every six students in your group.

For "Step Into Conflict" cut yarn into nine long lengths.

LEADER TIP
for The Study

Because this topic can be so powerful and relevant to kids' lives, your group members may be tempted to get caught up in issues and lose sight of the deeper biblical principle found in The Point. Help your kids grasp The Point by guiding kids to focus on the biblical investigation and by discussing how God's truth connects with reality in their lives.

Resolution   37

LEADER TIP for The Study

Whenever groups discuss a list of questions, write the list on newsprint and tape the newsprint to a wall so groups can discuss the questions at their own pace.

THE STUDY

EXPRESSIVE OPENING ▼

The Big Fight (5 to 10 minutes) After everyone has arrived, give the two actors you talked to before the study the signal to begin their argument.

After they have argued for about a minute, say: **Break it up. Please calm down and sit on the floor.** Ask the group:
● **How does it make you feel when others argue?**
● **Have you ever been involved in a conflict like this? If so, what happened?**
● **How do you usually react when others make you angry?**
● **What's the best way to respond when others make you angry?**
● **How could these two teenagers have better responded to their feelings?**

Say: **Before this meeting, I asked these two students to stage an argument to remind you that <u>sometimes Christians disagree.</u> As long as we're human, we will encounter conflict. There are times when we should try to avoid conflict, but there are also times when we must face it and work through it. Today we're going to look at the feelings surrounding conflict and discuss ways to deal with it. But before we begin, would someone please start our investigation with prayer?** Have a volunteer pray.

LEADER TIP for The Big Fight

Don't worry if other students get involved in the argument. Use the intrusion as an opportunity to help kids understand the emotions that surround conflict. Ask questions such as "Why did you get involved in the conflict?" and "How did the argument make you feel?"

Fight Feelin' (10 to 15 minutes)

Have kids form groups of six. Give each group one of the containers of mud you prepared before the study, and give each student a sheet of newsprint. Say: **I'd like each person to use the mud and the newsprint to create a picture that shows how conflict feels to you. The picture can be very detailed or very symbolic. Please don't get any mud on anything except your own hands and your own sheet of newsprint. You may *not* clean off your hands—even when you're done with your picture.**

Allow kids about seven minutes to create their pictures. While kids work, explain that they're allowed to make pictures of whatever emotions are involved when they experience conflict. Remind them not to wash or wipe the mud from their hands at any time.

When students are finished, give them the opportunity to present their pictures. Then ask:
● **How is conflict like your murals? different?**
● **How is conflict like your muddy hands? different?**
● **How does this activity demonstrate how you feel when you have a conflict with a friend?**

LEADER TIP for Fight Feelin'

You may want to put plastic on the floor or conduct this activity outdoors to protect the floor.

Resolution 38

● **How does this activity demonstrate why it's important to deal with conflict?**

Say: **Your hands are a physical representation of how many of us feel when we are involved in conflict. Conflict with others can make us feel dirty and gross. The longer we avoid dealing with it, the more difficult it becomes to get rid of the dirty and gross feelings. <u>Sometimes Christians disagree.</u> If we don't deal with the disagreements, our relationships or even our feelings about ourselves become negative and muddy. Working through conflict is a lot like washing the mud from our hands.**

Instruct kids to wash their hands.

LEADER TIP for Fight Feelin'

If your kids won't have access to a sink, provide buckets of water and towels for students to use to wash their hands.

KINETIC EXPLORATION ▼

Step Into Conflict (20 to 30 minutes) Have kids form three groups. Give each group a "Conflict Scenarios" handout (p. 42), a sheet of paper, a pen, and three long lengths of yarn. Assign a different scenario to each group. Say: **Each group has been assigned a situation that would probably lead to conflict. With your group, prepare a short skit that demonstrates the events following the situation. You will read your scenario to the class and will then present your skit. Try to demonstrate the thoughts and feelings that accompany the conflict.**

Everyone in your group must participate in the skit. To do this, you can either add characters that aren't mentioned in the scenario or you can make "blob" characters. To make a blob character, have two or more people stand together, and tie a length of yarn around the blob. All the people within the yarn circle act as one character but can take on different roles. For example, one

---

DEPTH FINDER — UNDERSTANDING CONFLICT

In an article titled "A Crash Course in Conflict" found in Leadership Journal (Fall 1996), Gary Fenton points out three essential aspects related to conflict:

● "There is a difference between concerned disagreement and conflict. Conflict is a disagreement that keeps decisions from being made or the group from moving forward after the decision has been made."

● "There is a difference between reconciliation and resolution. Resolution means finding an answer. Reconciliation means bringing the folks in conflict together. Some issues will never be resolved, but people can still be reconciled."

● "There is a difference between being peaceful and being a peacemaker...Peacemakers do not sit on their hands but often are in the middle of conflict, seeking to reconcile leaders."

Point out these differences to your kids. Showing kids that there are many issues involved in resolution will broaden their understanding of the difficulty in conflict and will better prepare them for encountering it.

Resolution

> ## DEPTHFINDER
> ### UNDERSTANDING CONFLICT IN GOD'S WORD
>
> "Some time later Paul said to Barnabas, 'Let us go back and visit the brothers in all the towns where we preached the word of the Lord and see how they are doing.' Barnabas wanted to take John, also called Mark, with them, but Paul did not think it wise to take him, because he had deserted them in Pamphylia and had not continued with them in the work. They had such a sharp disagreement that they parted company. Barnabas took Mark and sailed for Cyprus, but Paul chose Silas and left, commended by the brothers to the grace of the Lord" (Acts 15:36-40).
>
> Paul and Barnabas had a strong disagreement over what seemed to be a simple issue. The Bible doesn't say who was in the wrong or even if either of them were in the wrong.
>
> We do know that God used the conflict for good. As *Eerdmans Handbook to the Bible* explains, "The dispute over Mark results in two missionary journeys instead of one. Barnabas' special gift of encouragement no doubt helped his young nephew to make the grade and win Paul's approval later." As Paul tells Timothy at a later time, "Get Mark and bring him with you, because he is helpful to me in my ministry" (2 Timothy 4:11b).
>
> When your kids feel exasperated or overwhelmed because of conflict, direct them to Acts 15:36-40 and 2 Timothy 4:11b. Remind them that God is with them in the midst of conflict and that he can even use it to complete his purposes.

person can be the character's audible voice, and others can speak the character's thoughts aloud. You'll only have five minutes to prepare, so work quickly, and make your skits short and to the point.

Give kids about five minutes to prepare their skits. Have each group read its scenario and present its skit. Then ask:

● **What about the responses you presented makes them improper responses to conflict?**

● **How does it feel when others respond to you in those ways?**

● **How does God want us to respond to conflict?**

Give each group a copy of the "Resolution" handout (p. 43) and a pen. Say: **There's a better way to work through conflict. Let's present our skits again. But this time, use the tactics and verses on your handout to help you prepare a skit that shows a proper way to work through conflict. You have ten minutes to work through the handout and prepare your skit.**

After ten minutes, have each group present its skit. After each skit, ask:

● **Do you think this skit was realistic? Why or why not?**

After all the skits, ask:

● **Why does the Bible put such emphasis on working out conflict in private?**

● **Why does the Bible put such emphasis on resolving conflict quickly?**

● **What should you do if you are using the proper tactics for conflict resolution but the person you're dealing with refuses to do so?**

● Do you think the resolution tactics on the handout are practical? Why or why not?

Say: **God knows that <u>sometimes Christians disagree.</u> So he gave us tools and abilities to work through those disagreements. It's important to remember that not all conflict is bad. Sometimes two people can hold two very different, yet valid, opinions. All deep and lasting relationships go through conflict. If conflict is handled properly, it can actually strengthen a relationship.**

Tangled Up in Conflict (5 to 10 minutes)

Have kids get into groups of five. Have each group sit in a circle, and give each group a ball of yarn. Say: **Only the person who has the yarn may speak. After the person with the yarn is done speaking, he or she must wrap the yarn around his or her arm or leg and pass the ball of yarn to whoever speaks next.**

Instruct kids to allow each group member to talk about a conflict he or she has had or a current conflict that still needs to be resolved. Ask kids to refrain from talking a second time until everyone has had a chance to talk. Warn kids about gossiping, and encourage them not to use names if the people involved are common acquaintances. Have groups discuss the following questions while still using the yarn as an indicator of who is talking:

● **What causes conflict?**
● **Has this study changed the way you'll handle conflict? Explain.**
● **How is the tangle we're now in similar to a relationship that's in conflict?**
● **What do you think is the most effective way of avoiding a tangled mess when you have an argument?**

Give each group a pair of scissors. Read Matthew 18:15-17 aloud. Say: **When we follow what God tells us in his Word, we see that resolving conflict is necessary and possible. Through God's Word we see that even though <u>sometimes Christians disagree,</u> our relationships can survive and even flourish in the midst of conflict. If you're willing to attempt to work through conflict, show everyone else by cutting yourself out of the yarn tangle now.**

conflict scenarios

SCENARIO 1

Brenda is having a hard time in school. She's failing two subjects. She confided in Mark, her best friend, about the trouble she is having. One day, while Mark was talking to another friend, he accidentally brought up Brenda's difficulties.

Your assignment: Create a short skit that shows what happens when Brenda and Mark meet *after* Brenda discovers that he let her secret out. Finish the story with an improper response to conflict such as verbally attacking or avoiding.

scenario 2

Marcus had studied all night for the English exam. During the test, Rick whispered to Marcus to get help on a tough question. Marcus ignored Rick, so Rick whispered again. After hearing Rick's second whisper, Mr. Kirch ripped up both Marcus' and Rick's tests. Mr. Kirch has a zero-tolerance policy for cheating.

Your assignment: Create a short skit that shows what happens when Marcus explains to Mr. Kirch what happened. Finish the story with an improper response to conflict such as yelling or whining.

scenario 3

You and your sister are riding with your parents after church. As you are going to a restaurant, your sister begins to hit you with her seat belt. You respond by throwing one of your shoes at her. After a while, the disagreement escalates into both of you throwing punches, pulling hair, and pummeling each other.

Your assignment: Create a short skit that shows what happens when you and your sister are at the height of your argument. Finish the story with an improper response to conflict like blame or holding feelings in.

Resolution

Read Matthew 5:21-26 and Matthew 18:15-17. List all the things these verses show **we should do** and another list that shows all the things **we should avoid** when it comes to conflict.

Use the two lists you created and the following conflict-resolution tactics to demonstrate proper handling and resolution of conflict.

- **Prayer**—Seek God's direction before you say anything. Ask God to direct your conversation and to help you avoid saying something you'll regret.

- **Confrontation**—It's important that you go to the person you have the conflict with. Go to the person, and kindly express what you think the problem is. Use "I feel" statements rather than "You did/are" statements to explain why you are upset.

- **Listening**—It's important that you really listen to the other person's perspective. Try to put yourself in his or her shoes. Let the person know that you are trying to understand his or her viewpoint.

- **Resolution**—As you talk, offer and ask for options that can resolve the difficulty that you've had. Work toward a resolution both of you can live with.

- **Reconstruct**—Take some time to re-establish a relationship with the person you fought with. Ask the person to join you for lunch or something else you both enjoy.

THE ISSUE: Spiritual Gifts

the power within

Helping Kids Share Their Gifts

BY DEBBIE GOWENSMITH

■ "Young people are not attracted so much by a church that tries to entertain them as they are attracted to a church that challenges them to do things for others," says Tony Campolo in *Ideas for Social Action*. Unfortunately, many church members respond with a doubtful shrug: "I'm not sure our teenagers are interested in serving others." ■ What do teenagers say? Well, according to *A Student's Guide to Volunteering*, ten million high school and college students volunteer each year. One avid teenage volunteer says, "I've helped register voters. I've emceed a local youth conference. I've volunteered at the hospital. And I've loved every minute of it...I have daily opportunities to see God change the lives of other people. What could be more exciting than that?" (Campus Life, November/December 1996). ■ Could your church use that kind of enthusiasm? ■ Often the only barriers to teenage service in the church are a lack of encouragement, opportunities, or confidence. Kids wonder, "Can I really make a difference? Am I smart enough? strong enough? old enough? good enough?" ■ Give your kids a resounding "Yes!" Use this study to help them understand that they have special gifts to use. Excite them with the knowledge that through them, God can accomplish great things in the church.

THE POINT:

You have a gift to give.

The Study AT A GLANCE

SECTION	MINUTES	WHAT STUDENTS WILL DO	SUPPLIES
Group Solutions	10 to 15	THE POWER OF ONE—Attempt to solve problems in the church by using one spiritual gift.	Bible, newsprint, marker, tape
	15 to 20	THE POWER OF MANY—Attempt to solve problems in the church by using many spiritual gifts.	Bibles, "Gifts Committees" handouts (p. 53), scissors, newsprint, markers, paper, pens
Individual Exploration	15 to 20	THE POWER IN ME—Answer a questionnaire to help them begin to recognize their own gifts.	"The Power in Me" handouts (pp. 54-55), pens
Individual Commitment	5 to 10	THE POWER OF ACTION—Commit to using some of their gifts.	Bibles, construction paper, markers, tape

notes:

THE POINT OF "THE POWER WITHIN":

You have a gift to give.

THE BIBLE CONNECTION

ACTS 8:26-40; 18:24-28; HEBREWS 11:1-6; JAMES 2:14-17 — These passages demonstrate or explain specific spiritual gifts.

EPHESIANS 4:11-16 — This passage explains why Christians receive spiritual gifts.

1 PETER 4:10-11 — This passage encourages Christians to use their gifts for God's glory.

In this study, kids will form committees to explore how spiritual gifts can affect the church. Then kids will answer a questionnaire to help them recognize their own gifts. Finally, kids will commit to putting their gifts into action.

Through this exploration and commitment, kids can learn that as members of the body of Christ, they have the power of the Holy Spirit within them—and that with that power, they can contribute special gifts to the church.

Explore the verses in The Bible Connection; then examine the information in the Depthfinder boxes throughout the study to gain a deeper understanding of how these Scriptures connect with your young people.

BEFORE THE STUDY

For the "Power of One" activity, write the following challenges on newsprint, and tape the newsprint to a wall:
- The congregation hasn't had a new member in ten years.
- No one has remembered to visit sick church members for six months.
- The Bible confuses people, so they study the Sunday cartoons instead.
- People are starting to doubt whether God really cares at all.

LEADER TIP for The Study

Because this topic can be so powerful and relevant to kids' lives, your group members may be tempted to get caught up in issues and lose sight of the deeper biblical principle found in The Point. Help your kids grasp The Point by guiding kids to focus on the biblical investigation and by discussing how God's truth connects with reality in their lives.

THE STUDY

> **LEADER TIP**
> **for The Power of One**
>
> If you have more than twenty-five kids in your group, you can have kids form eight groups instead of four. Alter the activity by giving each challenge to two groups.
>
> If you have fewer than twelve kids in your group, you can have kids form two groups. Alter the activity by having each group solve two challenges.

> **LEADER TIP**
> **for The Power of One**
>
> If kids complain about the difficulty of the task you've given them, encourage them to just try harder. Then in the debriefing section, give them an opportunity to vent their frustrations with questions such as these:
> ● Why didn't trying harder help you complete your assignment?
> ● Why are the methods we use for solving problems more important than how hard we try?

GROUP SOLUTIONS ▼

The Power of One (10 to 15 minutes) After kids have arrived, have them gather around you. Say: **For the first activity today, you're all going to play the parts of members of different churches. Each of your churches is facing a serious challenge, and each of you has been elected to a church committee to solve the problem. In addition to being church members and committee members, you all have one more fundamental thing in common: You think that if people were simply giving more money, all of your churches' problems would be solved.** Have kids form four groups to create the following church committees: Giving Committee 1, Giving Committee 2, Giving Committee 3, and Giving Committee 4.

Point to the newsprint you taped to the wall before the study. Assign each committee a different challenge, and tell kids that they have to solve the problem through a plan based on giving money. Then say: **In a couple of minutes, the four committees will gather to learn what each has decided to do. Before then, your committee must not only solve the problem; it also must prepare a brief presentation to describe your solution to the other committees. But there's a catch: In your presentation, you may use only your arms to communicate—not your hands, mouths, feet, or anything else—just your arms. Begin.**

After a couple of minutes or when most of the groups have given up, call the committees back together. Have each committee present its

> **DEPTH FINDER** — **THE HOLY SPIRIT'S ROLE IN SPIRITUAL GIFTS**
>
> In Luke 24:49, Christ promised his disciples that they'd be "clothed with power from on high." Then, during Pentecost, the Holy Spirit came upon the disciples (Acts 2:4).
>
> Empowered by the Holy Spirit, the disciples accomplished great things. The Holy Spirit taught through the disciples (Acts 4:8-12), healed the sick through the disciples (Acts 14:8-10), and even raised the dead through the disciples (Acts 9:40). The Holy Spirit, by giving gifts to the disciples, established the body of Christ, the church.
>
> Acts 2:38-39; 5:32; 15:8; and 1 Corinthians 6:19 explain that Christians receive the Holy Spirit. And the Holy Spirit brings spiritual gifts. So spiritual gifts are not talents, not magic, and not powers to be attributed to human beings. They are gifts from the Holy Spirit that are to be used to accomplish God's purposes.

The Power Within   48

solution as best it can, and applaud after each presentation. Then say: **Based on what you had to work with, you all did a great job.** Have kids form new groups of four, with one person from each committee, to answer the following questions:

* **Was presenting solutions using only your arms frustrating or fun? Explain.**
* **What would have made the presentations easier?**
* **Was finding solutions based solely on giving money difficult or easy? Explain.**
* **What would have made finding solutions easier?**
* **How was using only your arms like or unlike using only the gift of giving to solve problems?**

Ask a volunteer to read aloud Ephesians 4:11-16. Then have kids discuss these questions in their foursomes:

* **Why do you think Christ gives gifts?**
* **Why do you think Christ uses different people to fill different roles in the church?**
* **How is the model given in Ephesians 4:11-16 like or unlike the way you tried to solve your church's challenges?**
* **How did our attempts to solve different problems using only one gift show why God gives us many different gifts?**

Say: **Just as our arms, legs, hearts, and brains work together to make our bodies function, the different spiritual gifts from Christ work together to benefit the body of Christ, the church. You have a gift to give, so let's learn what it might be and how you can use it.**

The Power of Many (15 to 20 minutes)

Have kids re-form the four committees from the first activity. Say: **You have a gift to give, though Christ may work through you in different ways to address different problems. In your committee, you're going to tackle the challenge listed on the newsprint again. This time, though, you're going to use a variety of gifts instead of just the gift of giving.** Assign each group one of the following committee names: Evangelism Committee, Faith Committee, Service Committee, and Teaching Committee.

Hand each committee its section of the "Gifts Committees" handout (p. 53). Tell committees they have ten minutes to complete the assignments on their handouts and to prepare their presentations. Set out Bibles, newsprint, markers, paper, and pens for groups to use. Circulate among the committees as they work, offering ideas or help as needed.

After ten minutes, call everyone back together. Have each committee present its solution and plan, and applaud after each committee has finished.

Then have kids form groups of four comprised of people who weren't on their committees. Ask them to discuss these questions:

* **Compared to the first activity, was finding and presenting solutions easier or more difficult? Why?**
* **How was presenting the solutions without physical restrictions like or unlike using a variety of gifts to benefit the church?**

LEADER TIP for The Study
Whenever groups discuss a list of questions, write the list on newsprint and tape the newsprint to a wall so groups can discuss the questions at their own pace.

LEADER TIP for The Power of Many
If you adapted the first activity in the study, you can adapt this one accordingly.

LEADER TIP for The Power of Many
The four spiritual gifts illustrated in this activity were chosen because they may be less intimidating and confusing to junior high students than some of the other gifts. As kids continue their study of Scripture and learn to develop and use their spiritual gifts, help them discover others.

The Power Within   49

LEADER TIP for The Power of Many

For future reference, you may want to compile a spiritual gifts notebook. Create a different section for each gift, include the appropriate section of the "Gifts Committees" handout (p. 53), and note what the committees learned about the purpose of each gift and their ideas for each gift. Make the notebook available to your students for personal study. As kids learn to use their gifts, write down their accomplishments in the notebook. Don't forget to add other gifts as kids learn about them.

● **How do spiritual gifts help the church function?**

Say: **Through helping to solve your church's problems, I hope you discovered more about spiritual gifts because you have a gift to give.**

INDIVIDUAL EXPLORATION ▼

The Power in Me (15 to 20 minutes)

Have kids remain in their foursomes, and say: **Now that we've learned a little bit more about spiritual gifts, let's try to help each other discover the gifts we may have.** Have kids tell the others in their groups the good qualities or gifts they think each group member might have. Then have each person find a place in the room to be alone. Hand everyone a copy of the "Power in Me" handout (pp. 54-55) and a pen. Give kids ten minutes to complete their handouts; then have them return to their foursomes to discuss these questions:

● **What's your reaction to this questionnaire?**
● **Did this questionnaire give you any new information about yourself? Explain.**
● **Does that information seem accurate? Why or why not?**

DEPTH FINDER — UNDERSTANDING THESE KIDS

In *The Religious Life of Young Americans*, George H. Gallup Jr. lists six basic needs of young people:
● the need to believe that life is meaningful and has a purpose,
● the need for a sense of community and deeper relationships,
● the need to be appreciated and loved,
● the need to be listened to—to be heard,
● the need to feel that one is growing in faith, and
● the need for practical help in developing a mature faith.

Gallup goes on to explain that by encouraging voluntarism and service, the church can help meet those needs: "Our young people sustain the American instinct towards voluntarism and acts of charity. Of course they like to have a good time, but if you want to draw more young people to your religious youth group, nothing can match the appeal of giving them the opportunity to donate their time, energy and enthusiasm to the community."

Kids are motivated to serve others. The most successful youth groups teach their kids to serve, Gallup says. "As they discover their differences, they are aided in developing their gifts in the service of God. The young are accepted in the church for what they are and can be, not simply for what we want them to be. They are given increasing responsibility and are encouraged to pour their energy into the affairs of the church and its service to society."

What a wonderful partnership! Teaching kids about their spiritual gifts—and then encouraging them and giving them opportunities to use their gifts—will meet your kids' needs *and* your church's needs.

The Power Within   50

Say: **To help you think even more about your spiritual gifts, answer these questions silently, and make notes on your handouts if you want to:**

- **What qualities do you most admire or respect about other people?**
- **Do you see some of those qualities in yourself? Explain.**
- **What are some things people who know you well say you're good at?**
- **Have you ever worked really hard at something and still felt energized? If so, what?**
- **What do you think a Christian's most important job is?**
- **What are some other ways you may be able to find out what your gifts are?**
- **What do you think is more important: figuring out what your gifts are or using them? Explain.**

Say: <u>**You have a gift to give,**</u> **and I hope you've learned a little more about what your gifts might be. But there's still another step to this process.**

INDIVIDUAL COMMITMENT ▼

The Power of Action (5 to 10 minutes) Have kids open their Bibles to 1 Peter 4:10-11, and ask a volunteer to read the verse aloud. Ask:

- **What does this Scripture say about what we should do with our gifts?**
- **Why do you think it's so important for us to use our gifts?**

Say: **God gives us gifts so we can use them to serve others and build up the church. Our gifts are worthless if they go unused.** <u>**You have a gift to give,**</u> **and you can start using it right now.**

Hand each person four sheets of colorful construction paper. On the first sheet, have everyone use a marker to write, "I have a gift to give" and sign his or her name. Then have kids tape these sheets of paper in a couple of rows along the bottom of a wall. Say: **God gives us gifts to build up his church. From the smallest to the grandest, God wants us to use our gifts.**

Ask kids to think of three goals—one immediate, one short-term, and one long-term—for using their gifts. Explain that they should be able to accomplish their immediate goals before they leave class, their short-term goals during the following week, and their long-term goals during the following month. Have kids use a separate sheet of construction paper to either draw a symbol of each goal or to write each goal. Then have them sign their names as a sign of their commitment to each goal.

After everyone has finished, tell kids that they have two minutes to accomplish their immediate goals. After everyone has accomplished that goal, have each person tape the sheet of construction paper that symbolizes that goal above the other taped-up sheets of construction paper. Ask:

- **Was it difficult or easy to think of goals? Explain.**

LEADER TIP for The Power of Action

If kids have difficulty setting immediate goals, offer suggestions such as praying for a friend, giving someone encouragement, or studying a passage of Scripture.

LEADER TIP for The Power of Action

If you don't have access to a wall where you can post long-term decorations, have kids write their goals on colored index cards and tape them in a notebook as they are completed. Bring the notebook to future meetings to remind kids to use their gifts.

The Power Within   51

DEPTH FINDER: WHAT ARE MY GIFTS?

The Discipleship Journal devoted an issue to the subject of spiritual gifts (issue ninety, 1995). In an article titled "Discovering Your Spiritual Gifts," Kenneth Cain Kinghorn presents the following six ways to discover your gifts:
- Open yourself to God as a channel for his use.
- Examine your aspirations for Christian service and ministry.
- Identify the needs you believe to be most crucial in the life of the church.
- Evaluate the results of your efforts to serve and to minister.
- Follow the guidance of the Holy Spirit as he leads you into obedience to Christ.
- Remain alert to the responses of other Christians.

In the same issue, David Henderson explains, "Say one of you owned a set of tools. Would you spend all your time counting them, naming them, organizing them, polishing them, putting them on display? Would you not simply use them? And so it is with the gifts of the Spirit: they are tools not to admire, but to use" ("Paul's Letter to Midvale Church").

Caution your kids against using the identification of their gifts as an excuse for waiting to serve. Challenge kids to become involved in serving—wherever it may be—to help them identify and grow in the gifts God has given them.

- **Is it difficult or easy to use our gifts? Explain.**

Say: **We started with a blank wall, and now we have a colorful example of how our accomplished goals build up the church. As you achieve your other goals, we'll continue to tape up your sheets of construction paper as reminders that <u>you have a gift to give</u> and that those gifts make a difference in the church.** Collect kids' sheets of construction paper, and put them in a safe place so kids can post their sheets as they accomplish their goals.

Over the next few weeks, remind kids of their goals. At the beginning of meetings, be sure to post sheets of construction paper that represent accomplished goals.

GIFT COMMITTEES

Evangelism Committee
1. Read Acts 8:26-40.
2. Discuss these questions:
   - What does it mean to evangelize?
   - How can evangelism be used to build up the church?
3. Brainstorm ways to use the gift of evangelism to address this challenge: The congregation hasn't had a new member in ten years.
4. Create a plan that uses the gift of evangelism to address that challenge. Use the provided supplies to present your plan.

Faith Committee
1. Read Hebrews 11:1-6.
2. Discuss these questions:
   - What does it mean to have faith?
   - How can faith be used to build up the church?
3. Brainstorm ways to use the gift of faith to address this challenge: People are starting to doubt whether God really cares at all.
4. Create a plan that uses the gift of faith to address that challenge. Use the provided supplies to present your plan.

Service Committee
1. Read James 2:14-17.
2. Discuss these questions:
   - What does it mean to serve God and others?
   - How can serving be used to build up the church?
3. Brainstorm ways to use the gift of service to address this challenge: No one has remembered to visit sick church members for six months.
4. Create a plan that uses the gift of service to address that challenge. Use the provided supplies to present your plan.

Teaching Committee
1. Read Acts 18:24-28.
2. Discuss these questions:
   - What does it mean to teach others?
   - How can teaching be used to build up the church?
3. Brainstorm ways to use the gift of teaching to address this challenge: The Bible confuses people, so they study the Sunday cartoons instead.
4. Create a plan that uses the gift of teaching to address that challenge. Use the provided supplies to present your plan.

The Power in Me

Complete this questionnaire to start thinking about how the Holy Spirit may want to work through you for the benefit of the church. This exercise deals with the spiritual gifts we're talking about in class today, plus four more; it does not include all the gifts.

This is *not* a test with right or wrong answers. Remember that this survey is designed to help you begin to think about your spiritual gifts.

Answer each question on a scale of 1 to 5.
1 = never; 2 = rarely; 3 = sometimes; 4 = often; 5 = always

Questions	Questions	Points	Gift
1. I like to help people who are weary or frustrated to feel better. _____	6. People like to talk to me about their problems. _____		A
2. I feel a strong need to tell others about Jesus Christ. _____	7. I like to invite people to church activities. _____		B
3. I know God can take care of any situation, no matter how bad things get. _____	8. When it comes to my beliefs, I follow my heart instead of my brain. _____		C
4. I give freely to others because I know that God will meet my needs. _____	9. I really enjoy giving my time and money to others. _____		D
5. When I'm with a group of people, I like to take charge. _____	10. My friends look to me to make decisions for the group. _____		E

Permission to photocopy this handout from Group's Core Belief Bible Study Series granted for local church use.
Copyright © Group Publishing, Inc., P.O. Box 481, Loveland, CO 80539.

Questions	Questions	Points	Gift
11. When I see disadvantaged people, I feel very sympathetic. _____	14. I am patient with people who have problems and try to help them. _____		F
12. I don't mind helping others with work even if I won't get any credit. _____	15. My friends tell me I'm very helpful. _____		G
13. I make a point to study the Bible regularly. _____	16. I really enjoy sharing what I learn with others. _____		H

After you've answered the questions, add your responses for each row, and record the answer in the "points" column. For example, if you answered question 1 with a "3" and question 6 with a "4," you'd write "7" in the "points" column.

Read the explanation of the spiritual gifts below. You may want to pay particular attention to the gifts for which you scored 6 to 10 points. Remember: This is not a test to tell you what your spiritual gifts are. It is a tool to help you think about your role in the church.

A. Encouragement—The Spirit-given ability to support others, giving them courage and hope.

B. Evangelism—The Spirit-given ability to tell others about Jesus Christ and help them know Jesus personally.

C. Faith—The Spirit-given ability to unquestioningly believe in God and to believe that God always does what is best.

D. Giving—The Spirit-given ability to give time and money where it's needed.

E. Leadership—The Spirit-given ability to motivate others to do work for the Lord.

F. Mercy—The Spirit-given ability to comfort people without judging them.

G. Service—The Spirit-given ability to assist and serve others.

H. Teaching—The Spirit-given ability to clearly and accurately relate God's Word and truth.

(Informational sources: Team Ministry's "Youth Spiritual Gifts Inventory," published by Church Growth Institute; and Discipleship Journal's special spiritual gifts section, issue ninety, 1995.)

why Active and Interactive Learning works with teenagers

Let's Start With the Big Picture

Think back to a major life lesson you've learned.
Got it? Now answer these questions:
- Did you learn your lesson from something you read?
- Did you learn it from something you heard?
- Did you learn it from something you experienced?

If you're like 99 percent of your peers, you answered "yes" only to the third question—you learned your life lesson from something you experienced.

This simple test illustrates the most convincing reason for using active and interactive learning with young people: People learn best through experience. Or to put it even more simply, people learn by doing.

Learning by doing is what active learning is all about. No more sitting quietly in chairs and listening to a speaker expound theories about God—that's passive learning. Active learning gets kids out of their chairs and into the experience of life. With active learning, kids get to *do* what they're studying. They *feel* the effects of the principles you teach. They *learn* by experiencing truth firsthand.

Active learning works because it recognizes three basic learning needs and uses them in concert to enable young people to make discoveries on their own and to find practical life applications for the truths they believe.

So what are these three basic learning needs?
1. Teenagers need action.
2. Teenagers need to think.
3. Teenagers need to talk.

Read on to find out exactly how these needs will be met by using the active and interactive learning techniques in Group's Core Belief Bible Study Series in your youth group.

1. Teenagers Need Action

Aircraft pilots know well the difference between passive and active learning. Their passive learning comes through listening to flight instructors and reading flight-instruction books. Their active learning comes

Helpful Stuff 57

through actually flying an airplane or flight simulator. Books and lectures may be helpful, but pilots really learn to fly by manipulating a plane's controls themselves.

We can help young people learn in a similar way. Though we may engage students passively in some reading and listening to teachers, their understanding and application of God's Word will really take off through simulated and real-life experiences.

Forms of active learning include simulation games; role-plays; service projects; experiments; research projects; group pantomimes; mock trials; construction projects; purposeful games; field trips; and, of course, the most powerful form of active learning—real-life experiences.

We can more fully explain active learning by exploring four of its characteristics:

- **Active learning is an adventure.** Passive learning is almost always predictable. Students sit passively while the teacher or speaker follows a planned outline or script.

In active learning, kids may learn lessons the teacher never envisioned. Because the leader trusts students to help create the learning experience, learners may venture into unforeseen discoveries. And often the teacher learns as much as the students.

- **Active learning is fun and captivating.** What are we communicating when we say, "OK, the fun's over—time to talk about God"? What's the hidden message? That joy is separate from God? And that learning is separate from joy?

What a shame.

Active learning is not joyless. One seventh-grader we interviewed clearly remembered her best Sunday school lesson: "Jesus was the light, and we went into a dark room and shut off the lights. We had a candle, and we learned that Jesus is the light and the dark can't shut off the light." That's active learning. Deena enjoyed the lesson. She had fun. And she learned.

Active learning intrigues people. Whether they find a foot-washing experience captivating or maybe a bit uncomfortable, they learn. And they learn on a level deeper than any work sheet or teacher's lecture could ever reach.

- **Active learning involves everyone.** Here the difference between passive and active learning becomes abundantly clear. It's like the difference between watching a football game on television and actually playing in the game.

The "trust walk" provides a good example of involving everyone in active learning. Half of the group members put on blindfolds; the other half serve as guides. The "blind" people trust the guides to lead them through the building or outdoors. The guides prevent the blind people from falling down stairs or tripping over rocks. Everyone needs to participate to learn the inherent lessons of trust, faith, doubt, fear, confidence, and servanthood. Passive spectators of this experience would learn little, but participants learn a great deal.

- **Active learning is focused through debriefing.** Activity simply for activity's sake doesn't usually result in good learning. Debriefing—evaluating an experience by discussing it in pairs or small groups—helps focus the experience and draw out its meaning. Debriefing helps sort and order the information students gather during the experience. It helps learners relate the recently experienced activity to their lives.

The process of debriefing is best started immediately after an experience. We use a three-step process in debriefing: reflection, interpretation, and application.

Reflection—This first step asks the students, "How did you feel?" Active-learning experiences typically evoke an emotional reaction, so it's appropriate to begin debriefing at that level.

Some people ask, "What do feelings have to do with education?" Feelings have everything to do with education. Think back again to that time in your life when you learned a big lesson. In all likelihood, strong feelings accompanied that lesson. Our emotions tend to cement things into our memories.

When you're debriefing, use open-ended questions to probe feelings. Avoid questions that can be answered with a "yes" or "no." Let your learners know that there are no wrong answers to these "feeling" questions. Everyone's feelings are valid.

Interpretation—The next step in the debriefing process asks, "What does this mean to you? How is this experience like or unlike some other aspect of your life?" Now you're asking people to identify a message or principle from the experience.

You want your learners to discover the message for themselves. So instead of telling students your answers, take the time to ask questions that encourage self-discovery. Use Scripture and discussion in pairs or small groups to explore how the actions and effects of the activity might translate to their lives.

Alert! Some of your people may interpret wonderful messages that you never intended. That's not failure! That's the Holy Spirit at work. God allows us to catch different glimpses of his kingdom even when we all look through the same glass.

Application—The final debriefing step asks, "What will you do about it?" This step moves learning into action. Your young people have shared a common experience. They've discovered a principle. Now they must create something new with what they've just experienced and interpreted. They must integrate the message into their lives.

The application stage of debriefing calls for a decision. Ask your students how they'll change, how they'll grow, what they'll do as a result of your time together.

2. Teenagers Need to Think

Today's students have been trained not to think. They aren't dumber than previous generations. We've simply conditioned them not to use their heads.

You see, we've trained our kids to respond with the simplistic answers they think the teacher wants to hear. Fill-in-the-blank student workbooks and teachers who ask dead-end questions such as "What's the capital of Delaware?" have produced kids and adults who have learned not to think.

And it doesn't just happen in junior high or high school. Our children are schooled very early not to think. Teachers attempt to help kids read with nonsensical fill-in-the-blank drills, word scrambles, and missing-letter puzzles.

Helping teenagers think requires a paradigm shift in how we teach. We need to plan for and set aside time for higher-order thinking and be willing to reduce our time spent on lower-order parroting. Group's Core Belief Bible Study Series is designed to help you do just that.

Thinking classrooms look quite different from traditional classrooms. In most church environments, the teacher does most of the talking and hopes that knowledge will transmit from his or her brain to the students'. In thinking settings, the teacher coaches students to ponder, wonder, imagine, and problem-solve.

3. Teenagers Need to Talk

Everyone knows that the person who learns the most in any class is the teacher. Explaining a concept to someone else is usually more helpful to the explainer than to the listener. So why not let the students do more teaching? That's one of the chief benefits of letting kids do the talking. This process is called interactive learning.

What is interactive learning? Interactive learning occurs when students discuss and work cooperatively in pairs or small groups.

Interactive learning encourages learners to work together. It honors the fact that students can learn from one another, not just from the teacher. Students work together in pairs or small groups to accomplish shared goals. They build together, discuss together, and present together. They teach each other and learn from one another. Success as a group is celebrated. Positive interdependence promotes individual and group learning.

Interactive learning not only helps people learn but also helps learners feel better about themselves and get along better with others. It accomplishes these things more effectively than the independent or competitive methods.

Here's a selection of interactive learning techniques that are used in Group's Core Belief Bible Study Series. With any of these models, leaders may assign students to specific partners or small groups. This will maximize cooperation and learning by preventing all the "rowdies" from linking up. And it will allow for new friendships to form outside of established cliques.

Following any period of partner or small-group work, the leader may reconvene the entire class for large-group processing. During this time the teacher may ask for reports or discoveries from individuals or teams. This technique builds in accountability for the teacherless pairs and small groups.

Pair-Share—With this technique each student turns to a partner and responds to a question or problem from the teacher or leader. Every learner responds. There are no passive observers. The teacher may then ask people to share their partners' responses.

Study Partners—Most curricula and most teachers call for Scripture passages to be read to the whole class by one person. One reads; the others doze.

Why not relinquish some teacher control and let partners read and react with each other? They'll all be involved—and will learn more.

Learning Groups—Students work together in small groups to create a model, design artwork, or study a passage or story; then they discuss what they learned through the experience. Each person in the learning group may be assigned a specific role. Here are some examples:

Reader

Recorder (makes notes of key thoughts expressed during the reading or discussion)

Checker (makes sure everyone understands and agrees with answers arrived at by the group)

Encourager (urges silent members to share their thoughts)

When everyone has a specific responsibility, knows what it is, and contributes to a small group, much is accomplished and much is learned.

Summary Partners—One student reads a paragraph, then the partner summarizes the paragraph or interprets its meaning. Partners alternate roles with each paragraph.

The paraphrasing technique also works well in discussions. Anyone who wishes to share a thought must first paraphrase what the previous person said. This sharpens listening skills and demonstrates the power of feedback communication.

Jigsaw—Each person in a small group examines a different concept, Scripture, or part of an issue. Then each teaches the others in the group. Thus, all members teach, and all must learn the others' discoveries. This technique is called a jigsaw because individuals are responsible to their group for different pieces of the puzzle.

JIGSAW EXAMPLE

Here's an example of a jigsaw.

Assign four-person teams. Have teammates each number off from one to four. Have all the Ones go to one corner of the room, all the Twos to another corner, and so on.

Tell team members they're responsible for learning information in their numbered corners and then for teaching their team members when they return to their original teams.

Give the following assignments to various groups:

Ones: Read Psalm 22. Discuss and list the prophecies made about Jesus.

Twos: Read Isaiah 52:13–53:12. Discuss and list the prophecies made about Jesus.

Threes: Read Matthew 27:1-32. Discuss and list the things that happened to Jesus.

Fours: Read Matthew 27:33-66. Discuss and list the things that happened to Jesus.

After the corner groups meet and discuss, instruct all learners to return to their original teams and report what they've learned. Then have each team determine which prophecies about Jesus were fulfilled in the passages from Matthew.

Call on various individuals in each team to report one or two prophecies that were fulfilled.

You Can Do It Too!

All this information may sound revolutionary to you, but it's really not. God has been using active and interactive learning to teach his people for generations. Just look at Abraham and Isaac, Jacob and Esau, Moses and the Israelites, Ruth and Boaz. And then there's Jesus, who used active learning all the time!

Group's Core Belief Bible Study Series makes it easy for you to use active and interactive learning with your group. The active and interactive elements are automatically built in! Just follow the outlines, and watch as your kids grow through experience and positive interaction with others.

> **FOR DEEPER STUDY**
>
> For more information on incorporating active and interactive learning into your work with teenagers, check out these resources:
>
> ● *Why Nobody Learns Much of Anything at Church: And How to Fix It,* by Thom and Joani Schultz (Group Publishing) and
> ● *Do It! Active Learning in Youth Ministry,* by Thom and Joani Schultz (Group Publishing).

your evaluation of

Bible Study Series
for junior high/middle school

the truth about
THE CHURCH

Group Publishing, Inc.
Attention: Core Belief Talk-Back
P.O. Box 481
Loveland, CO 80539
Fax: (970) 669-1994

Please help us continue to provide innovative and useful resources for ministry. After you've led the studies in this volume, take a moment to fill out this evaluation; then mail or fax it to us at the address above. Thanks!

• • • • • •

1. As a whole, this book has been (circle one)

not very helpful   very helpful
1   2   3   4   5   6   7   8   9   10

2. The best things about this book:

3. How this book could be improved:

4. What I will change because of this book:

5. Would you be interested in field-testing future Core Belief Bible Studies and giving us your feedback? If so, please complete the information below:

Name _____

Street address _____

City _____ State _____ Zip _____

Daytime telephone (____) _____ Date _____

THANKS!

Permission to photocopy this evaluation from Group's Core Belief Bible Study Series granted for local church use.
Copyright © Group Publishing, Inc., P.O. Box 481, Loveland, CO 80539.